YOUR KNOWLEDGE HAS VALUE

- We will publish your bachelor's and master's thesis, essays and papers

- Your own eBook and book -
  sold worldwide in all relevant shops

- Earn money with each sale

Upload your text at www.GRIN.com
and publish for free

Samantha Lack

Faithful Harry and the Reformation

Evaluating Events Leading to Henry VIII's Excommunication

GRIN Publishing

Bibliographic information published by the German National Library:

The German National Library lists this publication in the National Bibliography; detailed bibliographic data are available on the Internet at http://dnb.dnb.de .

This book is copyright material and must not be copied, reproduced, transferred, distributed, leased, licensed or publicly performed or used in any way except as specifically permitted in writing by the publishers, as allowed under the terms and conditions under which it was purchased or as strictly permitted by applicable copyright law. Any unauthorized distribution or use of this text may be a direct infringement of the author s and publisher s rights and those responsible may be liable in law accordingly.

Imprint:

Copyright © 2011 GRIN Verlag, Open Publishing GmbH
Print and binding: Books on Demand GmbH, Norderstedt Germany
ISBN: 978-3-656-23745-7

This book at GRIN:

http://www.grin.com/en/e-book/194093/faithful-harry-and-the-reformation

GRIN - Your knowledge has value

Since its foundation in 1998, GRIN has specialized in publishing academic texts by students, college teachers and other academics as e-book and printed book. The website www.grin.com is an ideal platform for presenting term papers, final papers, scientific essays, dissertations and specialist books.

Visit us on the internet:

http://www.grin.com/

http://www.facebook.com/grincom

http://www.twitter.com/grin_com

Faithful Harry and the Reformation:
Evaluating Events Leading to Henry VIII's Excommunication.

Samantha Lack

October 27, 2011

Henry VIII has been evaluated numerous times by historians over the centuries since his death. He is a figure in history that has the power to awe those who study him. One reason for the wonderment that surrounds the studies of Henry VIII was his ever-changing philosophies. He was a king that appreciated knowledge and was a devout Catholic but that all changed in the 1520s, and from that time on, his viewpoints about religion and his status in England began to resemble that of a crazed man. Events in Henry's life helped shape the type of king he would change into. Early in his reign he defended the Catholic Church with his *Seven Sacraments* and not too many years later, he was Supreme Head of the English Church. Henry's life choices changed him and all of England.

To understand Henry as a person, one must understand the times into which Henry was born. He was born on June 28, 1491 at Greenwich Palace, to Henry VII, King of England, and his queen, Elizabeth of York. The War of the Roses was a recent memory and the Tudor dynasty was still yet to be firmly established. There is little known about his childhood and this was probably due to the fact that he was the second son. In the late 15th century, the oldest son was the one destined to take the throne once the king passed away. For this reason, Henry's older brother Arthur was the son that was documented most as a child.[i] Henry was intended for a life in the church. Because of this, Henry had a great knowledge of the canon and could often quote appropriate scriptures when occasions arose.[ii]

In October of 1501, Henry's older brother, Arthur, married Catherine of Aragon of Spain. The marriage was not the success that Henry VII hoped for because in April of 1502 Arthur died. For a brief moment, Henry VII considered taking Catherine as his wife (his wife, Elizabeth of

York, had recently died), and this was better than returning the dowry that had come to England with Catherine. To solve the matter Henry VII arranged a marriage between his son, Henry, the new Prince of Wales, and Catherine. Some in the English Church did not look upon the proposed marriage favorably, and it was suggested that Henry VII request a bull of dispensation from Julius II (the current pope) to allow the Prince of Wales to marry his deceased brother's wife.[iii] Julius II granted the dispensation in 1503 but the marriage between Henry and Catherine did not happen until 1509, after Henry VII had died and Henry VIII was of appropriate age.[iv]

With his secluded youth behind him, Henry loved his pastimes. He kept close friends, such as Charles Brandon, and was always active. The new king of England was hailed as a divine prince, one who had mastered sports, arts, language, music, canon law, and who was most learned. He was a new kind of prince and was much admired by the greats during his time. Men, such as Erasmus, praised him and were certain that Henry was bringing in a new, and improved, age to England.[v] With his extracurricular activities filling his time, he did not have much interest in the day-to-day operations of England. This job eventually fell on his chief minister, Cardinal Wolsey.

On January 1, 1511, a baby was born to Henry and Catherine. There had been a previous pregnancy but it resulted in a stillborn daughter. This time, the child was alive, and it was a son. The boy was named Henry, after his father, and was given the title the Prince of Wales. Henry and Catherine celebrated in lavish style, but, as was common during this time in history, the boy died early at seven weeks. Henry and Catherine were both devastated.[vi] Catherine became pregnant two additional times following this but both pregnancies resulted in deceased sons. Henry and Catherine began to lose hope that they would ever have living children, and worst of all, no stable heir for the throne of England. Finally, in February of 1516, Catherine gave birth to their fifth child, a healthy, screaming, active, baby girl. Henry and Catherine named her Mary.

The birth of their daughter renewed their spirits. Henry believed that if they could have a healthy daughter, there was still hope for a healthy son. Catherine became pregnant again in 1518, and London began to buzz about the prospect of finally having a male heir. Unfortunately, a daughter was born and died within a week. This would be Catherine's last pregnancy. Out of six pregnancies, only a daughter survived, and unfortunately, she was not the depiction of a secure heir that Henry preferred.[vii]

Henry's attention was directed toward the religious upheaval that was happening around Europe. Martin Luther had posted his *Ninety-Five Theses* condemning the actions of the Catholic Church in 1517. Luther was a Catholic but believed that the church was full of debauchery.[viii] By 1519, Luther's works were known all over Europe and places like Oxford were beginning to flow with his followers. The next year Luther wrote *The Babylonian Captivity of the Christian Faith*, which was an attack on the Catholic Church and it's holy sacraments. Henry was enraged that Luther was gaining momentum. Believing that he was a faithful follower and servant of God, Henry crafted his defense of the Church. When Henry finished his *Assertio Septem Sacramentorum (The Defense of the Seven Sacraments)*, he sent several copies to the papacy. He also wrote the pope saying, "Nothing is more the duty of a Christian prince than how to preserve the Christian religion against his enemies."[ix] In his *Defense,* Henry wrote, "He [Luther] so undervalues Customs, Doctrine, Manners, Laws, Decrees and Faith of the church…that he almost denies there is any such thing as a church, except perhaps such a one as himself makes up of two or three heretics, of whom himself is chief."[x] Partially in reward for Henry's defense of the papacy, the pope rewarded Henry with a new title, "The Defender of the Faith". It should be noted that the title was not only given for Henry's work on his *Defense*. Henry and Wolsey had been working with the papacy for several years trying to gain a title for

Henry that would match the holy titles that had been bestowed on other Christian princes in Europe.[xi]

When Luther read Henry's published *Defense*, he initially did not believe that Henry was the authentic author nor did he believe that it was a satisfactory argument. Luther responded to the *Defense* in his *Martinus Lutherus contra Henricum Regem Angliæ*,

> The sum of the matter is: the whole of Henry's book is based on the words of men, and on the use of centuries, and on no words of God, nor on any use of the Spirit. On the contrary, the sum of my argument is that whereas the words of men, and the use of centuries, can be tolerated and endorsed, provided they do not conflict with the sacred Scriptures, nevertheless they do not make articles of faith, nor any necessary observances.[xii]

Luther was challenging Henry's *Defense* and Henry realized that Luther's teachings were a threat, not only to the papacy, but also to him as a king. Luther and Henry exchanged writings and they both strongly believed the other was misguided. In 1525, Luther and Henry were still exchanging letters, and Luther apologized to Henry for doubting his authorship of his *Defense*. Henry was very quick to reassure Luther that he did not need, or desire, his apology.

The year 1525 also saw another big event, the completion of William Tyndale's New Testament translation. Henry, upon writing to the German princes in 1523 to request the restraint of Luther, was quoted as saying, "It is a good thing for the Scriptures to be read in all languages."[xiii] This was not a common belief among the Catholic Church and Henry did not accept his own words as true. He was writing what he thought the German princes wanted to hear in order to get them to heed to his request. Unfortunately for Henry, his tactics did not work and Luther continued to be safe in Germany.

The Catholic Church looked down upon commoners reading Scripture. The hierarchy of the church believed that "special knowledge" was required to understand the Scriptures. When

Wyclif's Bible was published in the early fifteenth century, the church reacted by forbidding any version of the Bible to be written without episcopal approval. Tyndale did not have the approval of the bishops to translate his version. He had once told a friend of his intentions to translate the Bible and his friend believed that it was better "to be without God's law, than without the pope's." Tyndale answered, "If God spare me life, ere many years I will cause the boy that driveth the plow to know more of the Scripture than you do."[xiv] Tyndale spent six months in London translating his Bible from Hebrew to English and then traveled to Germany to finish the first portion of his work under the influence of Luther. When the king tried to hush the excitement surrounding Tyndale's translation by having him arrested, Tyndale escaped and managed to finish his translation of the Old Testament. Eventually, Tyndale was captured and burned at the stake as a heretic in 1536. His last words were, "Lord, ope the King of England's eyes".[xv]

During Henry's reign he had many foes. The first foe he found was Ferdinand of Spain, his father-in-law. On many occasions Ferdinand did not keep his promises to help the young Henry in battle, and as a result, this caused Henry much humiliation during a time that he was trying to establish his power. Two successive French kings also caused Henry much grief. They were Louis XII and, his son, Francis I. As was common during the early sixteenth century, Henry signed multiple peace treaties with both men. Both sides would pledge their unyielding affection for the other and promise loyalty, at least until a better offer came from a more influential adversary.

Henry's biggest rival during his lifetime was Charles V of Spain. Early in 1519, the Holy Roman Emperor (Maximilian I) died. His grandson, Charles V, and the French king, Francis I, started competing for the title of Holy Roman Emperor. Henry was more willing to support Charles while Wolsey preferred Francis. Both candidates received assurances that they had England's support by way of money, letters, and false promises. In the beginning of the campaign for Emperor, Henry was not interested in earning the title for himself. Suddenly Henry decided to add his name to the campaign list. It is not known if Henry was serious about his attempt to gain this new title. The possibility exists that he was trying to split the votes between Charles and Francis. But adding the title of Holy Roman Emperor to Henry's designation would have created a tremendous amount of power and prestige for the king. Henry had his ambassador, Richard Pace, visit the electors and campaign for him. All of Pace's work was to no avail and in June of the same year, Charles was elected Emperor. Charles was now the most powerful prince in Europe, both King of Spain and Holy Roman Emperor.[xvi]

  Before Charles was crowned emperor, he had made a treaty with England to marry Henry and Catherine's daughter, Mary. Because of this fact, Henry was not threatened that Charles had become emperor. Instead he was excited about the prospect of his daughter being empress and the Holy Roman Empire joining England through marriage. Henry was gravely disappointed then, when Charles dissolved the marriage treaty. Mary was only a child of nine years old at this time and Charles was ready to marry. He had no desire to wait until she came to a marriageable age. Charles chose Isabella of Portugal as his new bride. It also helped that Isabella came with a dowry of one million crowns. Once again Henry and England were rebuffed.[xvii]

  Henry's first known mistress was a young and beautiful girl by the name of Elizabeth Blount, also known by her nickname Bessie.[xviii] Bessie was a teenager when she first caught the eye of the king during New Year celebrations at court.[xix] Bessie was so appreciated by the king that she became his official mistress for several years. During this time, Catherine was still having trouble producing a living heir for England. It must have been heart-wrenching news to Catherine when Bessie bore Henry a son in 1519. The child was named Henry Fitzroy and given his own household and the title of Duke. Henry was relieved to finally have a living son, though he was not legitimate and did not have a solid entitlement to the throne. For Catherine the birth of Henry Fitzroy only hardened relationships between her and Henry. In Henry's eyes, Bessie's son was proof that Henry could produce living male heirs, leaving the blame entirely on Catherine.

Henry's next mistress was Mary Boleyn, the wife of William Carey. Little was known about their relationship and it has been rumored that she bore Henry another son, although there is no evidence to show that to be true. Henry and Mary's relationship lasted several years but was over by the mid-1520s.[xx] By this time, another Boleyn lady caught the eyes of the king, and she proved to be a temptation too much for Henry to bear.

Anne Boleyn was a young woman, at the age of eighteen or nineteen, when she came to court as a lady in waiting for Catherine in 1526. She was not a notably beautiful woman but nevertheless, Henry took notice of her. Anne was no stranger to court matters. She had spent three years as a teenager in the French court of Queen Claude and she knew of her sister's relationship with Henry. From the beginning it was clear that Anne had a power over Henry. He desired her sexually and promised to be devoted to her, if only she agreed to become his official mistress. She said no. Perhaps she did not want to have a fate similar to her sister or perhaps she was striving for a more noble title, but when she denied Henry, it put him into a fury. Had she accepted, it is possible that, "She would have been used and discarded."[xxi] He had to have her for his own and there was not much he would not do in order to accomplish his desire.[xxii]

In 1526, two big changes happened to Henry that altered the course of English history. The first, and probably most important, was his new attitude about his responsibilities as king. From the beginning of his reign he had his advisors, especially Thomas Wolsey, take care of the state matters. Secondly, Henry met Anne, and she denied the offer of official mistress.[xxiii] Catherine was now out of her childbearing years and therefore had no hope of providing England with a suitable heir. Henry was desperate. "He had a deep and passionate desire for a male heir, a desire which, in an age before any woman had sat on the English throne, was natural and comprehensible."[xxiv] Henry saw his new love Anne as the only possible way to have a legitimate heir. But there was the problem of Catherine.

Henry first contemplated divorcing Catherine in 1514, after several failed pregnancies.[xxv] His hope was renewed when Mary was born, and survived, but another failed pregnancy followed, resulting in a stillborn daughter. Henry began to believe that his marriage to Catherine had offended God. According to Leviticus 20:21, it was forbidden for a man to take his brother's wife, and if a man did so, the couple would remain childless. Even though Henry and Catherine had a healthy daughter, they did not have a son, and in Henry's eyes, that meant they were "childless".

Another event that allegedly shook Henry's confidence was the questioning of Mary's legitimacy by the French ambassador in 1527. After more than one failed attempt to achieve a marriage for his daughter, Henry was looking at the possibility of aligning England with France with Mary's marriage to the French king's second son, the Duke of Orleans.[xxvi] Scarisbrick notes that "It is incredible that an ambassador would have dared to trespass upon so delicate a subject as a monarch's marriage…Nor was it likely that he should have suggested that Mary was illegitimate when her hand would have been very useful to French diplomacy." It is more likely that Henry or Wolsey fabricated the story, or that the ambassador had been requested to raise such a question by Henry to gives grounds for his annulment.[xxvii] Whatever the real reason behind Henry's desire for a divorce, he was determined to see his marriage end, and make Anne his new queen.

It was decided that Wolsey would ask the king to answer charges on the validity of his marriage to Catherine. By having Wolsey as the instigator to the annulment, Henry felt that he was less likely to have a tarnished reputation when the matter was settled. "He needed to convince himself that separation from Catherine would not compromise his standing, and his self-image, as a virtuous Christian prince."[xxviii] Catherine pleaded to Rome and her nephew, Emperor Charles, for help in defending her status as queen and true wife of Henry. A secret court was enacted in England but nothing significant was accomplished. It was decided that Henry should appeal his case to the pope, since Julius II had provided the bull of dispensation allowing the marriage in 1503.

The first sign that Henry's case was not proceeding according to plans was on May 6, 1527, when Emperor Charles sacked Rome and took Pope Clement VII as his prisoner. Wolsey knew Pope Clement VII must be liberated or he would never rule in favor of Henry.[xxix] At this point, Henry, becoming more desperate with time passing, changed what he wanted. He was willing to keep Catherine as his wife, if he could get a dispensation from the pope for bigamy, and marry Anne as well. With Wolsey's persistence against this matter, Henry dropped this petition and requested another. He returned to his request for an annulment and wanted a dispensation from the pope stating that he could marry Anne, so long as his annulment was granted. This was required because of his conjugal relations with Anne's sister, Mary. "In seeking such a dispensation he betrayed to the pope the real object of his activities; he thus disclosed that his real purpose was to marry Anne Boleyn and not to ease his conscience, and thereby rendered the papacy suspicious of his good faith in the matter."[xxx]

With the papacy suspicious of Henry's intentions and the pope still the prisoner of the emperor, Henry's case was stalled. Clement VII desired to grant Henry his request but was unable to do so. Clement was a man of weak character, and with his neutrality in the case he earned the enmity of both Henry and Charles. Finally Clement decided to grant a decretal commission. The decretal commission allowed Cardinal Campeggio and Cardinal Wolsey to try the case in England. Campeggio was to show the commission to no one. Clement had instructed him to delay the proceedings in England for as long as possible and to not hand down a verdict until further instructions came.[xxxi]

The trial began in England on June 18, 1529. The high point of the trial was three days later when Henry addressed the court. He reassured the people in attendance that the trial was about the clearing of his conscience. He told them that he had been living in sin for eighteen years and God had punished him for it. After he completed his speech, Catherine came to him, got down on her knees, and pleaded with him. She begged for proper counsel and restated that she was a "true maid" when they married. When she was finished, she arose and left the court. Catherine was summoned back three times but refused every command. On July 23, Campeggio was expected to give his verdict, but instead, to the complete disgust of the king, he adjourned the court until October 1 to consult with the pope. That same month, after much pleading from Catherine, the pope granted Catherine the right to defend herself in the case. "A supreme egoist, Henry's capacity for believing in his own righteousness was almost unlimited, and that the pope should feel bound to consider the queen's claim to justice appeared to him as the blackest ingratitude."[xxxii] After this announcement by Clement, he further suspended the case until after Christmas. Campeggio left England at this point and Henry wrote to the pope all his complaints.[xxxiii]

Through his dealings with the annulment proceedings, Wolsey lost favor with the king. His fall was now certain. Henry called the Reformation Parliament to meet in England beginning on November 3, 1529. Among other matters, the Reformation Parliament considered the proposition of reducing the ecclesiastical power and wealth. In 1528, a gentleman by the name of Simon Fish had published a pamphlet called *The Supplication of the Beggars*. This pamphlet asked the king to take the lands and riches that belonged to the papacy in England. During this time, the papacy owned more land in England than any duke.[xxxiv] The last, and most important decision of the Reformation Parliament was the declaration to support Henry in his desire for a male heir. With Wolsey out of the picture, Henry's new advisor, Thomas More, sat in on the proceedings.[xxxv] The Reformation Parliament ended having achieved its goals but the divorce issue was still far from over.

Henry was by this point close to giving up on his case. He was quoted as saying, "[I] would never have sought a divorce had [I] not been assured that papal authority might easily be obtained."[xxxvi] At this moment, two men entered the scene that would assist the king in achieving his ideal end. Thomas Cranmer, a Cambridge man, was the first to raise the question of whether the king's divorce was not a law question but a matter of theology. When Henry heard of Cranmer's ideas, he took him into his service and requested that he put his views on paper.[xxxvii] Following this, Henry sent agents all over Europe to universities to get their opinion on whether the pope had the authority to allow a man to marry his brother's wife. The answers that came back were divided, but eventually the University of Paris provided Henry with the answer he desired. It was not long after this that Oxford and Cambridge followed suit.[xxxviii]

The other man to influence Henry's actions was Thomas Cromwell. Cromwell was "a man of large administrative skill, great ability and no moral scruples."[xxxix] Cromwell alluded to the idea that the papacy was the controlling agent in England, and that as king, Henry should be head over his territory (inhabitants and clergy). By Henry becoming the driving force in England, he would have the power to try the divorce case under a "true" English court. After hearing Cromwell's suggestions, Henry wrote the pope yet again. He pleaded with the pope to allow the case to be tried under English law. On January 5, 1531, Clement denied Henry his request. In the same brief, the pope forbade Henry to remarry under threats of excommunication.[xl]

Henry, under the influence of Cromwell, decided it was time to attack the clergy in England. Wolsey had died shortly before this time, and Henry had *praemunire* charges brought up on the remainder of the clergy. Henry desired that they plead guilty and that they recognize Henry as the Supreme Head of the Church of England. Chapuys is quoted as saying about *praemunire* charges that, "no person in England can understand, and its interpretation lies solely in the king's head, who amplifies it and declares it at his pleasure, making it apply to any case he pleases."[xli] The clergy met and decided to offer Henry 100,000 pounds but they would not acknowledge their guilt. Henry refused their offer. Eventually, after coercion by Henry's advisors, the clergy was convinced to accept their guilt along with paying Henry the money. They also approved his title, changing it to "Supreme Head of the English Church, so far as Christ Allows".[xlii]

Thomas More, Henry's advisor following Wolsey, was repulsed by the clergy's submission to Henry. More was not a supporter of the divorce but on March 30, 1531, he was charged with the job of reading the findings from the universities. After finishing, he was asked his opinion on the matter. He refused to give it.[xliii]

After many delays parliament finally met again on January 15, 1532. Cromwell was now in Henry's inner circle and Henry's policies reflected the ideas of Cromwell. One of the main items on the agenda was to do away with the first fruits that were sent to the papacy every year. In 1534, the clergy was forced to sign the Act of Submission of the clergy to Henry. This was the final act that took the power from the clergy to Henry. "With the presentation to the king of their Submission, the bishops ceased to be masters in their own house."[xliv] Thomas More, the king's trusty advisor, resigned from his post the day after the submission was signed.[xlv]

On August 23, 1532, William Warharm, the Archbishop of Cantebury died. He was the leading advocate for the papacy in England. Now that he was dead, Henry was free to choose his successor, one that would see to it that Henry's mission was accomplished. Henry appointed Thomas Cranmer. In April 1533, "The Acts of Restraint and Appeals" passed in England. This act completely removed the pope's authority in England. At this point, Henry and his parliament were now in charge.[xlvi]

With everything in place for Henry to finally have his divorce, the Duke of Suffolk and the Duke of Norfolk visited Catherine in that same month. She was advised that her case was now all but finished, that Henry and Anne were already married, and Anne was pregnant with Henry's child. In May, Cranmer opened the trial at Dunstable. Catherine received a summons to appear before the court but did not show. On May 23, 1533, Cranmer declared Henry's marriage to Catherine invalid. Cranmer then proceeded to declare Henry's marriage to Anne official. Cranmer's actions resulted in the declaration that Henry had never been married to Catherine, therefore, he had been free to marry Anne from the beginning.[xlvii] On July 11, the pope excommunicated Henry. He also said that Henry and Anne's marriage was invalid and any children they had would be illegitimate. He then advised Henry to take his true and lawful wife, Catherine, back. Henry ignored the pope's advice and believed that the child that Anne carried was his long awaited son.[xlviii] It was not. A daughter was born, whom they named Elizabeth.

Henry's excommunication did not end the English Reformation. There were still many events that followed that solidified Henry's new status. The Acts of Succession came in 1534, and it required all notables to take an oath that their allegiance was to Henry as head of the church and not the pope. Parliament also passed the Treason Act. It dealt with those that spoke against the king or those that refused to recognize him as Supreme Head. Thomas More, Henry's old advisor, resisted the Treason Act and stayed strong in his Catholic beliefs. More was executed for his defiance.[xlix]

The English Reformation was not a movement that concerned religion as was the Protestant Reformation that surrounded Luther and his followers. Henry's reform in England was based solely on his personal desires and his insecurity. Henry was apprehensive about his throne being passed to a daughter. He did not want all of his father's achievements with the War of the Roses to end with him. If the dynasty did end, and his daughter over-thrown as queen, he would be considered a failure. (The irony of the story was with all his worries about a daughter of his sitting on the throne; Anne's daughter, Elizabeth, became the greatest queen that England had ever known.) Henry was also insecure in his relationship with the papacy. For so long he tried to earn a title equal to other Christian princes in Europe. This was of great importance to him and when he did achieve the title of "Defender of the Faith" he finally felt like a worthy and noble Christian prince. Even after separating from the Catholic Church, Henry kept the title.

As of 1533, Henry had his beloved Anne and was Supreme Head of the Anglican Church. It had been a long road to arrive at this destination and Henry had sacrificed much and many. When he was excommunicated from the Catholic Church, Henry did not stop believing like a Catholic. He still believed in everything that the Catholic Church offered, minus the pope's authority. It was unlikely that Henry would have ever received the pope's permission for his divorce in a manner that suited him, so it was convenient for him to argue the pope's authority. Had the pope given his approval, there would have less reason for Henry to denounce him. Because Henry still held tight to his Catholic beliefs, he continued to persecute heretics, especially protestant ones, during the remainder of his reign.[l]

It can also be denounced that Anne was the sole cause of Henry's divorce. When Henry first began to entertain the idea of a divorce in 1514, Anne was a girl at the age of seven. By the time she arrived at court in 1526, Henry's affections for Catherine had long been gone. Henry stopped having conjugal visits with Catherine by 1524. "We may conclude that Henry's suit for annulment was accelerated, though hardly caused, by his infatuation with Anne."[li]

By examining the course of events it is evident that Henry's disgust with Catherine, infatuation with Anne and his arguments with the papacy, were all centered on the one constant in Henry's reign; his desire for a male heir. It would not be sufficient to have another bastard child. Having another bastard child like Henry Fitzroy would not solve his succession problem.[lii] Had Catherine provided Henry with a suitable heir, her position would have been more secure. She also would have been in a better position to battle Anne and Anne might have also been reluctant to encourage the king in his divorce. Anne knew the only reason Henry wanted a new queen was to provide a son. If Catherine had succeeded in her mission as queen, Anne's only use to Henry would have been as a mistress and England might have a very different history from that time on. Historians will never know what might have happened had Henry and Catherine had a son, but it is possible that Anne Boleyn might be a name that few would recall today and Henry might be remembered as an English king of not much significance, instead of, "Henry the Eighth, by the Grace of God, King of England, France and Ireland, Defender of the Faith and of the Church of England and also of Ireland in Earth Supreme Head".

Notes

---

[i] Jack Scarisbrick, <u>Henry VIII</u> (Los Angeles: University of California Press, 1968), 3.

[ii] Will Durant, <u>The Story of Civilization: The Reformation</u> (New York: Simon and Schuster, 1957), 523.

[iii] David Loades, Henry VIII:Court, Church, and Conflict (Richmond Surrey: The National Archives, 2007), 22.

[iv] Durant, 535-536.

[v] Loades, 18-38.

[vi] Scarisbrick, 27.

[vii] Carolly Erickson, Great Harry (New York: Simon & Schuster, 1980), 155.

[viii] Arthur D. Innes, England Under the Tudors (London: Methuen & Co. Ltd., 1950), 85.

[ix] Neelak Serawlook Tjernagel, Henry VIII and the Lutherans (Saint Louis: Concordia Publishing House, 1965), 3-7.

[x] Henry VIII, *Assertio Septem Sacramentorum* (New York: Benziger Brothers, 1908), Kindle edition.

[xi] Scarisbrick, 115-116.

[xii] "*Martinus Lutherus contra Henricum Regem Angliæ,*" Project Canterbury, accessed May 10, 2012, http://anglicanhistory.org/lutherania/against_henry.html.

[xiii] Tjernagel, 10-33.

[xiv] Durant, 533.

[xv] Ibid., 533.

[xvi] Scarisbrick, 98-105.

[xvii] Erickson, 167-173.

[xviii] Loades, 48.

[xix] Scarisbrick, 147.

[xx] Erickson, 159.

[xxi] Scarisbrick, 149.

[xxii] Ibid., 148-151.

[xxiii] Erickson, 186-187.

[xxiv] Geoffrey de Clinton Parmiter, The King's Great Matter: A Study of Anglo-Papal Relations 1527-1534 (London: Longmans, Green and Co LTD, 1967), 1.

[xxv] Durant, 536.

[xxvi] Giles Tremlett, Catherine of Aragon: The Spanish Queen of Henry VIII (New York: Walker Publishing Company, 2010), 225.

[xxvii] Scarisbrick, 153-154.

[xxviii] Tremlett, 227.

[xxix] Parmiter, 13-16.

[xxx] Ibid., 26-28.

[xxxi] Scarisbrick, 216.

[xxxii] Parmiter, 108-109.

[xxxiii] Ibid., 99-110.

[xxxiv] Durant, 543.

[xxxv] Parmiter, 116.

[xxxvi] Ibid., 143.

[xxxvii] Tjernagel, 68-71.

[xxxviii] Durant, 545.

[xxxix] Parmiter, 144.

[xl] Ibid., 144-149.

[xli] Ibid., 154.

[xlii] Ibid., 152-159.

[xliii] Ibid., 159-161.

[xliv] Ibid., 190-192.

[xlv] Scarisbrick, 300.

[xlvi] Parmiter, 195-223.

[xlvii] Ibid., 232-237.

[xlviii] Durant, 547.

[xlix] Parmiter, 287-298

[l] Durant, 549.

[li] Ibid., 537-538.

[lii] Loades, 52.

Works Cited

Durant, Will. *The Story of Civilization: The Reformation.* New York: Simon and Schuster, 1957.

Erickson, Carolly. *Great Harry.* New York: Simon & Schuster, 1980.

Henry VIII. *Assertio Septem Sacramentorum.* New York: Benziger Brothers, 1908. Kindle edition.

Innes, Arthur D. *England Under the Tudors.* London: Methuen & Co. Ltd., 1950.

Loades, David. *Henry VIII: Court, Church, and Conflict.* Richmond Surrey: The National Archives, 2007.

Parmiter, Geoffrey de Clinton. *The King's Great Matter: A Study of Anglo-Papal Relations.* London: Longmans, Green and Co LTD, 1967.

Project Canterbury. "*Martinus Lutherus contra Henricum Regem Angliæ.*" Accessed May 10, 2012. http://anglicanhistory.org/lutherania/against_henry.html.

Scarisbrick, Jack. *Henry VIII.* Los Angeles, CA: University of California Press, 1968.

Tiernagel, Neelak Serawlook. *Henry VIII and the Lutherans.* Saint Louis: Concordia Publishing House, 1965.

Tremlett, Giles. *Catherine of Aragon: The Spanish Queen of Henry VIII.* New York: Walker Publishing Company, 2010.

www.ingramcontent.com/pod-product-compliance
Lightning Source LLC
LaVergne TN
LVHW090150080526
838201LV00116BA/1548